Cancer

21 June – 21 July

amber
BOOKS

ASTROLOGICAL SIGN DATES:
The precise start and end times for each sign
vary by a day or two from year to year as
the Gregorian calendar shifts relative to the
tropical year. The dates provided in this book
are correct for the year 2020.

If you are unsure of the Zodiac sign
for your specific birth year, visit: www.
yourzodiacsign.com.

Cancer

21 June – 21 July

A guide to understanding yourself, your friendships and finding your true love

This edition first published in 2020 by
Amber Books Ltd
United House
North Road
London N7 9DP
United Kingdom
www.amberbooks.co.uk
Instagram: amberbooksltd
Facebook: amberbooks
Twitter: @amberbooks

ISBN: 978-1-83886-023-3

Project Editor: Sarah Uttridge
Design: Zoë Mellors

Picture Credits:
All illustrations by Fabbri Publications except the following:
Shutterstock: 31 (Elena Naumchenkova), 32 (La Puma), 35 (muuraa),
36 (Slonomysh), 40 (Angel Soler Gollonet)

Printed and bound in China

TRADITIONAL CHINESE BOOKBINDING
This book has been produced using traditional Chinese bookbinding
techniques, using a method that was developed during the Ming Dynasty
(1368–1644) and remained in use until the adoption of Western binding
techniques in the early 1900s. In traditional Chinese binding, single sheets
of paper are printed on one side only, and each sheet is folded in half,
with the printed pages on the outside. The book block is then sandwiched
between two boards and sewn together through punched holes close to
the cut edges of the folded sheets.

Contents

Introduction   6

The Elements   9
Colours of the Zodiac   12
The Angelic Hierarchy   14
The Genders   15
The Ruling Planets   17
The Qualities   20
Signs and Symbols   22
Cancer the Crab   25
The Sun in Cancer   27
Appearance   31
Health   32
Career   34
Relationships   37
Ideal Partner   40
Compatibility in Relationships   42
The Cancerian Child   44
Famous Cancerians   46
Finding your Sun Sign   48

Introduction

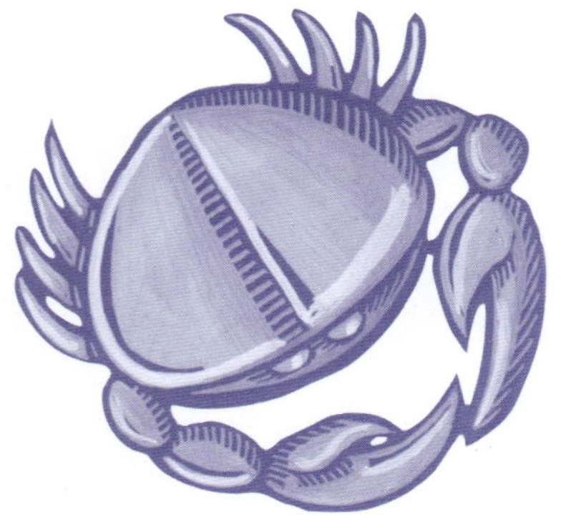

Cancer

21 June–21 July

Sign: The Crab

Ruling Planet: The Moon

Gender: Feminine

Element: Water

Quality: Cardinal

Compatibility: Taurus and well-aspected Leos

Non-compatibility: Capricorn and Pisces

Every man, woman and child is born with a distinct and different destiny. There are no exceptions. Everyone has cosmic significance and a part to play in the life of the universe. This is innate and inescapable, and goes beyond the tiny boundaries of nation, creed and colour.

As we live out our lives on planet Earth, we are, however unknowingly, acting in a greater drama and reacting to impulses that come from distant astronomical bodies, stars and planets millions of light years away. Sceptics pour scorn on the idea that far-distant Saturn, for example, can have any effect on our lives, as the ancient art and science of astrology teaches. But the fact is that we are sparks of energy inhabiting bodies made of the same stuff as the stars, responding like tiny radios to the distant messages they send to Earth.

Each infant carries within it a double blueprint for life: its genetic programming and the pattern of character that comes from the astrological 'clock' that was set in motion at the moment of birth. No one knows the full extent of genetic influence, although it seems to be astonishingly far-reaching, but the power of the horoscope has been well known to the wisest men and women for many centuries.

Our Sun signs provide essential inside information about our destinies. They reveal the secrets of who we really are and why we are here, laying out before us our potential, the sort of joys and achievements our characteristics may bring about, and warn us of problems to be overcome through the triumph of free will.

Read this book with an open mind and discover who you really are.

The Elements

Up to the beginning of the Age of Enlightenment – the modern scientific era – in the 18th century, it was commonly believed that everything, including human beings, was made up of the four elements: Earth, Air, Fire and Water. These were thought of as the building blocks of life, and each astrological sign had a predominance of one or another. Each created its common characteristics, although too much of any of the elements can produce an unbalanced personality.

Water Signs

The Water signs are Cancer, Scorpio and Pisces. They are emotional, intuitive and often psychic, strongly in touch with the hidden, mysterious side of life and with the ebb and flow of unseen energies. Like the ocean tides, they have surges of inspiration and bursts of euphoria, or they can be plunged into gloom and introspection. Cancerians are emotionally tied to their homes and families; like their sign, the Crab, they jealously guard their own particular little rock pool, hiding their softest feelings underneath a hard shell.

Scorpians are the occultists and profound thinkers of the zodiac, very sexy and magnetic, but sometimes too intense. They are the still waters that run deep – very, very deep.

Pisceans' emotions can lie undisturbed for long periods, then suddenly rise to the surface. They can be fast and elusive – slippery customers, sometimes – and change direction for no apparent reason, often against their own best interests. But, like the other two Water signs, they operate almost entirely through their feelings, which can be very positive when set against the dour practicality of a Capricornian or the most reliable investment banker of a Taurean. They give depth to the adventures of the Arian and the madcap schemes of the Geminian, and reveal some of the mysteries of the Universe.

Water Signs

Colours of the Zodiac

Traditionally, each sign of the zodiac has its own colour, which is believed to be 'lucky' or magically empowered for those born under that particular sign. In general, the colours are associated with the ruling planets and are symbolic of their attributes. Many people find that they feel most comfortable when wearing their sign's colours, and often choose them without knowing their astrological background.

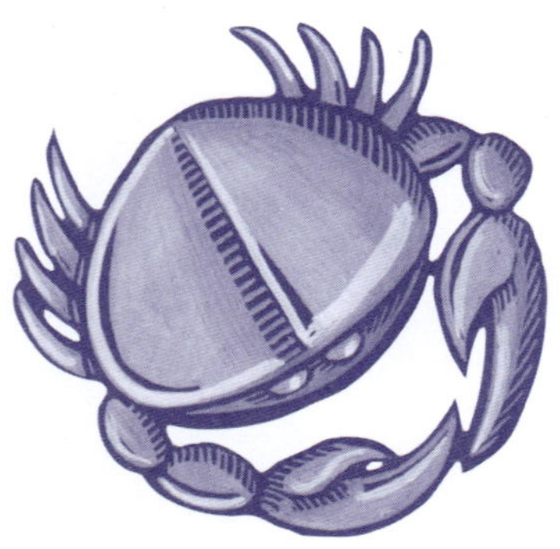

Cancer

Ruling Planet: the Moon.

Colours: Pale blue and silver.

These aid the flow of intuition and constructive and revelatory dreaming, and put Cancerians in touch with their secret, psychic selves. However, these colours can lead to unrestrained and inappropriate daydreaming. Cancerians must remember that the chores have to be done some time!

The Angelic Hierarchy

According to ancient tradition, each planet is governed by one of the great archangels, who are also rulers of certain aspects of human life. The box below lists the planet that they rule, the areas over which they have influence and their special day of the week.

Gabriel

Archangel of the Moon.

Governs: Cancer.

Rules: Femininity, intuition and all matters psychic.

Day: Monday.

The Genders

Traditionally, the twelve signs of the zodiac are divided into Masculine and Feminine, although of course both men and women are born into each.

The characteristics were assigned to the genders aeons ago, well before modern feminism or political correctness, and may now seem old-fashioned to many. However, the signs do seem to be grouped according to the appropriate gender.

The Feminine Signs

The Feminine signs are Taurus, Cancer, Virgo, Scorpio, Capricorn and Pisces. Feminine traits tend to be accentuated in the Water signs Cancer and Pisces.

These signs present gentler, more passive qualities. They are the carers and the nurturers, inclined to take a back seat and worry over the well-being of others. They are artistic and in tune with their intuition, and may be psychic. Self-evidently, these are the motherly and sisterly signs, with all the attendant positive and negative characteristics. They tend to be the power behind the throne, rather than movers and shakers, although many are great achievers, especially in the modern, more egalitarian world, where their qualities are encouraged.

Negatively, the Feminine signs can be fussy, possessive, mean-minded, vindictive, cringing, clinging and over-emotional.

Aquarius, the sign of the coming Age, is endowed with both Masculine and Feminine traits, although it is traditionally categorized as Masculine.

The Ruling Planets

Until the 18th century, astrologers knew only the planets of our solar system that could be seen with the naked eye: Mercury, Venus, Mars, Jupiter and Saturn. (For the purposes of astrology, the Sun and the Moon are also counted as planets even though the Sun is a star and the Moon is the satellite of Earth.) Uranus was discovered in 1781, Neptune in 1846 and Pluto was first seen in 1930. Many astrologers believe that the existence of other heavenly bodies – such as the rumoured Vulcan, which hypothetically exists within the orbit of Mercury – is about to be confirmed. Astrologers will then have to agree which signs these 'new' planets will rule, and what human characteristics their discovery will accentuate.

The Moon

The Sun's illumination gives the illusion that the Moon grows and diminishes in size or waxes and wanes, producing the three major phases of New Moon, Full Moon and Dark of the Moon. When the orbiting Moon completely masks the Sun, it creates the spectacular phenomenon of a solar eclipse. This is now thought to have limited astrological significance, although once, like the Moon itself, it was believed to have a major effect on human life.

However, the Moon does have a major role to play in the drama of life on Earth. It causes tides to ebb and flow, and induces certain types of behaviour in animals. The hatching of baby turtles, for example, takes place under a Full Moon. Many animals become restless and aggressive at this time. Research suggests that humans are similarly affected. Some people believe that sleeping in the light of the Full Moon helps women regulate their menstrual cycle. Some research indicates that the Moon affects plant life, both on land and in the depths of the oceans.

In mythology, the Moon is traditionally associated with women, whereas the Sun is honoured as a male god. The Moon is the Queen of Heaven, a title

About the Moon

The Moon orbits the Sun together with the Earth, and meanwhile also circles the Earth approximately once every 27.5 days.

The sacred day of the Moon is Monday.

also given to the Egyptian goddess Isis and, later, to the Virgin Mary. The Moon is associated with magic, spell-casting and seduction, which is why the other great lunar goddesses Circe and Hecate are considered to be enchantresses. So strong was the distrust of the latter's power by the early Church that she became associated with Hell. However, the ancient Egyptians also had a Moon deity: the goddess Tsukiyomi.

Cancerians are ruled by the Moon, which is believed to make them emotional, caring and nurturing, although they can become easily distressed and possessive. The Moon is traditionally associated with silver.

The Qualities

In addition to the influence of gender, the elements and the planets, each sign of the zodiac is affected by having an intrinsic quality – Cardinal, Fixed or Mutable.

Cardinal Quality

Those with a strong Cardinal quality to their chart are, traditionally, supremely ambitious and perhaps somewhat ruthless in getting to the top. They are bursting with ideas and are dynamic in pursuing their goals, especially where their careers are concerned. They see themselves as achievers and winners: every day is a challenge that they willingly accept. Their sense of determination inspires others, although they themselves will continue to take the lead and initiate every new project. They can be dismissive of lesser mortals. Cardinality also represents new beginnings.

Cancer

At first sight, this sign does not seem to fit the classic profile of Cardinality, being too unassertive and introverted. However, many Cancerians are courageous and determined fighters, although usually on behalf of others, especially their children.

Signs and Symbols

Most people are familiar with the zodiac 'zoo' – the collection of symbols that represent the twelve signs. These images reflect the characteristics traditionally assigned to each sign and contain a wealth of knowledge about its true nature.

Each sign of the zodiac is represented by a symbol – the twin fish for Pisces, for example. No one is sure exactly when or why the symbols were chosen, although some authorities believe they date from Sumeria or Mesopotamia, 4000 years before Jesus Christ. The priest-astrologers of the ancient world were the first to impose recognizable patterns on the great constellations – Leo the Lion being one example.

Today, seeing such shapes in the stars may seem fanciful, but thousands of years ago imaginations were more poetic, and many myths told of magical animals, such as the dragon, which had strange powers to influence everyday human life.

Although the ancient Egyptians left few astrological records, they were almost unique in antiquity for worshipping archetypal, animal-headed gods. However, these strange hybrid gods – half-human, half-animal – were worshipped as aspects of one God. Contrary to the general belief that the Egyptians were idolaters, their religion was basically monotheistic. Each statue represented an aspect of the one true God.

Since they were established, the signs have remained unchanged, although there was a movement in the Middle Ages to change the sign of Aquarius into the sign of John the Baptist – presumably because of the connection with water.

The twelve signs of the zodiac do seem particularly apt on the whole, and accurately reflect the archetypal character of Sun sign types. The great Swiss psychoanalyst Carl Gustav Jung (1875–1961) believed that, deep in our psyches, humanity shares a collective unconscious – a set of archetypal images, which, at a profound level, we all understand. The signs of the zodiac form part of this pool of images, conveying eternal truths to our unconscious minds.

Signs and Symbols

Cancer The Crab

The Crab is perhaps the least appropriate symbol in the zodiac. Whereas the small scuttling sea creature is a loner and scavenger, Cancerians are passionate about their families and immediate circle of friends. They can become upset and depressed if denied their company. More than any other sign, Cancerians need others in order to fulfil themselves and to satisfy their innate urge to be of service.

Crabs live half their lives in the water and half on the land, and, in a figurative sense, this is true of those born under the sign of Cancer, for they bring an intense awareness of the submerged, subconscious realm into the light of everyday reality. This, though, does not always make for an easy life. Too often, Cancerians feed off the psychic, intuitive and feminine aspect of the hidden mind and turn it into a constant demand for emotional satisfaction. However, the more well-balanced Cancerians have learned to tame this side of their character and to use their unique insights for the good of others.

Cancer

Cancerians possess the typical Water sign's emotional intensity, which is enhanced by being ruled by the Moon. Their moods often ebb and flow like the tides, and they frequently allow themselves to be carried away on a wave of feeling, trusting to fate that no harm will befall them.

Like the crab, those born under this sign tend to put up a protective front when their loved ones are threatened, or in order to conceal their own soft-heartedness. Some Cancerians become so frightened or embittered by life that they take to hiding behind their shells most of the time.

Of course, crabs, no matter how tiny, can give nasty nips with their claws, especially if cornered, and this describes the normally amenable Cancerian, who can lash out hurtfully if put on the spot.

There are no known mythological associations, but as the crab, in one form or another, was known to all ancient cultures, it may be assumed that its characteristics were generally agreed to fit those of the typical Cancerian.

There was a move to change the name of those born under this sign from Cancerians – because of the connotations arising from the disease of the same name – to 'Moon Children', but it failed to catch on.

The Sun in Cancer

Sun sign Cancerians are the most family-centred of the zodiac. Fiercely protective of their loved ones, they are nourishers and carers at heart. Loving, demonstrative and tender-hearted to the point of sentimentality, they attach great importance to anniversaries, trinkets and trips down memory lane. They are unashamedly feminine and even male Cancerians tend to be carers. Cancerians are also in tune with their true self and in touch with their intuition. They are often psychic and can be intuitively wise, but distrust cold logic and analysis: book learning for its own sake is not for them. Unlike fellow Water sign Pisces, Cancerian dreams are rarely vague and other-worldly, focusing instead on creating images of success and happiness for those they love. Though often without driving ambition for themselves, they yearn passionately on behalf of others. They are artistic, practical and excellent homemakers. The world outside rarely offers anything to eclipse the attraction of coming home, especially home to the family, and even lone Cancerians lavish time and money on creating their ideal.

However, those born under the sign of the Crab are great worriers, constantly fretting about the health and safety of their family and friends. As far as Cancerians are concerned, if someone is a few minutes late, something bad must have happened to them. Their constant fussing can drive others to distraction. So can their tendency to be over-emotional and sentimental, eyes brimming with tears for the slightest reason – whether real or imagined.

Cancerians take offence easily, often going off in a huff. They tend to fall out with others and then keep their distance. They may not speak to those

Personality traits of Cancerians

Positive	*Negative*
Protective	Worriers
Caring	Over-emotional
Intuitive	Sentimental
Loyal	Take offence
Artistic	easily
Practical	Bear a grudge
Excellent	Socially timid
homemakers	
Family-centred	

who have ruffled them, sometimes for years on end. Cancerians can also be tenacious. They hang on to a relationship, belief or cause with their crab's claws, even when it causes them pain. For them, it is enormously difficult to let go and move on. They are constantly looking back and can wallow in nostalgia, even though the past was not the golden age or romantic dream they seem to imagine. Cancerians are very good at creating their own myths and turning humdrum lives into fairy stories, even if it means being economical with the truth. Anyone who tries to make them face facts is answered with outrage, denial and a storm of hurt tears.

Being too emotional makes Cancerians moody, withdrawn and even secretive. Sometimes they can sulk for days, without being able to find out why. Since they are virtually telepathic, they find it hard to understand that others may not necessarily share their intuitive gifts.

Cancerians are both loving and loyal, but can be unsure of themselves and somewhat timid socially, preferring to give someone else the limelight. They will, however, shine at providing the refreshments after the star has done his or her turn.

Appearance

Cancerians are often smallish, with round 'moon' faces and a tendency to put on weight. This applies especially to women who may have what used to be described as a 'motherly figure'. These earth mother types have abundant, shiny hair, soulful eyes and are economical with their gestures. Another Cancerian type is thin and nervy, with red hair, and tends to be more extroverted in social conditions.

Some people born under the sign of the Crab become so sour through bitterness and worry that it is reflected in the permanent downturn of their mouths, their prematurely lined faces and their cold, dissatisfied expressions. On the whole, Cancerians move as little as possible and only a real emergency will make them move swiftly.

Health

Cancerians, the archetypal couch potatoes, are happiest slouching in front of the television. Exercise is generally anathema to them, but they can be encouraged to take part in family walks or other social but not too physically demanding

activities. However, being a Water sign, Cancerians can excel at watersports: even the most exercise-phobic among them will willingly take the plunge if there is a swimming pool nearby.

Cancerian weaknesses include their digestive systems, where all that worry can wreak havoc, causing heartburn, colitis and ulcers. Women tend to suffer from breast problems and water retention, but both men and women become very distressed by all illnesses, trivial as well as serious. They tend to become hypochondriacs, always visiting the doctor, on behalf of family members as well as themselves, and buying over-the-counter remedies. Many Cancerians are fascinated by holistic or alternative therapies, and can spend a fortune working their way through them. It is important to stress that those born under the sign of Cancer are not more likely than any other sign to develop the illness of the same name, but of course it is always a good idea to have regular health checks.

Career

Being naturally sympathetic, practical and nurturing, Cancerians make excellent nurses. They understand how unsettling illness can be, and easily relate to their patients. They are natural with children, especially tiny tots, and make memorable primary school and special needs teachers. Here their immense reserves of patience are often rewarded with remarkable progress. Their ability to sympathize with others who are in difficulties also attracts them to counselling and charity work. They can often be found working as volunteers on telephone hotlines, perhaps as suicide or AIDS counsellors. Cancerians are also the mainstay of help for the homeless and like to make donations for far-off victims of famines. They cannot bear the idea of anyone going hungry, and are the first to react to television images of skeletal babies in the developing world. However, although excellent at 'hands-on' charity work, they can often be far too sensitive and thin-skinned to work for any length of time in famine areas or with war victims. Most, with some notable exceptions, simply could not take the scale of the misery, nor the sights and smells of atrocities and human suffering.

Reliable and responsible, they make good co-workers but they can equally run their own small businesses. This is where being so organized with money helps. Cancerians also make imaginative

The best careers for Cancerians

- Nurse
- Teacher
- Counsellor
- Charity worker
- Chef
- Caterer
- Librarian
- Curator
- Researcher

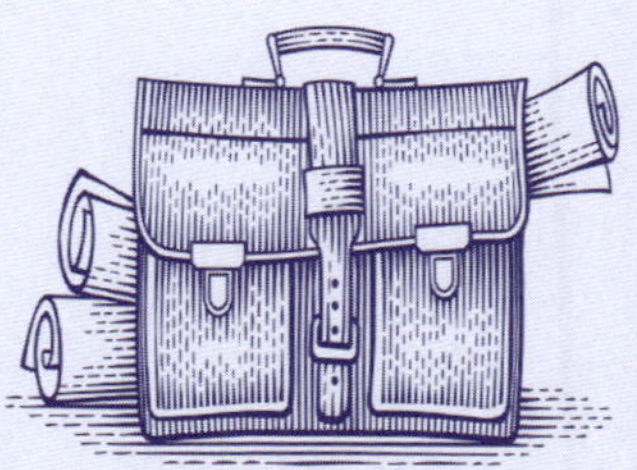

cooks and caterers, although they prefer to see people's reactions to their dishes rather than remaining behind the scenes in the kitchen. Because of their love of the past and tradition, you may find some Cancerians working in museums and libraries, or in the antiques trade. They also make tenacious researchers, especially in tracking down genealogical data or some fact of local history. They may have problems, though, with modern technology. Some are actually technophobes, something that can hamper the progress of their chosen careers.

Relationships

Cancerians make relationships their business, but they are sometimes not as good at it as they think. They make loving parents, sensitive lovers and generally docile children. However, Cancerians tend to smother their children, suffocating them and others with their endless fussing and their inability to accept that people need their own space and freedom. Children must have their own lives, but Cancerian parents, especially mothers, find that hard to accept. Cosseted and over-protected, children of typical Sun sign Cancerians can grow up timid and unadventurous or, conversely, become rebels.

Cancerians cling. Female Crabs often refuse to accept that a boyfriend doesn't love them any more or will not even consider marriage. With an over-romanticized image of love and marriage, it is inconceivable to them that the man in their life does not also want the cottage with roses around the door and two-point-four children playing with granny in the garden. Long after any hope of reconciliation, Cancerians are still trying to revive the long-dead embers of a relationship. They seem not to realize that endless scenes of tearful entreaty succeed only in pushing their beloved further away. They also cling to old-fashioned values, and even non-religious Cancerians may expect to be virgins on their wedding night. They may also expect their bride or groom to be equally unsullied.

Many Cancerians do not realize that they have the power to lash out and hurt others, though almost never in a physical way. When they are on the defensive – and they often are – Cancerians can hit back with very cruel words, often dredging up old secrets in order to inflict the greatest hurt. If faced with this aspect of their behaviour, they will either deny it utterly or berate themselves for being so wicked. On such occasions, it is better not to press for a rational discussion. When Cancerians are blinded by emotion, they will never see reason. Perhaps when they have calmed down, the topic can be raised in a more constructive manner. But even then it will have to be handled very sensitively. Many Cancerians can take constructive criticism, especially those whose professional training, perhaps in nursing or counselling, makes them more amenable to it. However, it is hard coming from loved ones, and often causes deep family or marital rifts. Cancerians long for an atmosphere of love and harmony to prevail in the home. However, they take every little criticism personally, and brood over it, possibly even for years, so that the hurt goes deep and is constantly fresh in their minds, while everyone else has forgotten about it.

Ideal Partner

Cancerians should stay clear of typical Sun signs who cannot cope with emotions, especially Capricornians, who tend to be wintry in the expression of their feelings. Best for them are steady, grounded types such as Taureans,

who can be very happy to create a nest with these traditional homebodies. They also understand the need to keep a firm hand on the bank balance, and this combination creates an almost ideally secure background in which their children can grow up and fulfil their real potential.

Idealistic Aquarians and canny Virgoans can also fit the bill, although they may find Cancerian emotionality very hard to take.

Proud Leos, however, could find Cancerians supportive. Cancerians may idolize them, easily falling into their role as nurturers rather than leaders. Badly aspected Leos can be overbearing and badly aspected Cancerians snivelling martyrs, which makes a bad mix. However, most are well balanced enough to make the combination work.

Compatibility in Relationships

Aries
20 March–19 April

The fire and dash of Aries appeals but they have little time for Cancerian emotion. It might work but not for long.

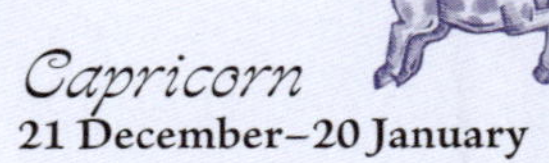

Capricorn
21 December–20 January

True Goats will never understand the Cancerian's need to discuss emotion, which will frighten them off for good.

Cancer
21 June–21 July

Though they have much in common, two emotional blackmailers under the same roof can make for disaster.

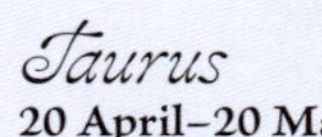

Taurus
20 April–20 May

This is a perfect match: both are homemakers and respecters of family values. They will enhance each other's lives.

Libra
23 September–22 October

Life can be easy for a while. Librans value their independence too much to hand it over to a Cancerian.

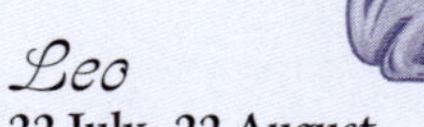

Leo
22 July–22 August

Cancerians can worship Leos and make fine homes with them. With enough compromise, an excellent match.

Scorpio
23 October–21 November

Flashy Scorpians may infatuate Cancerians, but the price is too high. One drama queen is enough!

Aquarius
21 January–18 February

Home-loving Cancerians feel threatened by real crusading Aquarians who want to change their settled world.

Gemini
21 May–20 June

Self-seeking and specious Geminians can be charm itself, but they'll never be a lifelong partner.

Virgo
23 August–22 September

This combination can work, though Virgoans may be puzzled and upset by Cancerian outbursts and contradictions.

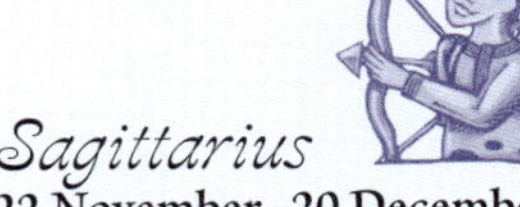

Sagittarius
22 November–20 December

Cancerians want to own their beloved's body and soul – the last thing a Sagittarian will ever agree to.

Pisces
19 February–19 March

Both Water signs can be tearful clingers, which is not the best recipe for lasting love or mutual respect.

The Cancerian Child

Hypersensitive and moody, the Cancerian child will be mummy's boy or daddy's girl from the cradle. Even so, they will love both parents to distraction and live in fear of being abandoned by them or even left alone. It is important for the adopted Cancerian child to be told as early as possible about his or her background. Leaving it until they are older may cause emotional upset.

Cancerians are inherently untidy, and this is made worse by their inability to throw anything away. Hoarding is second nature to them, due partly to a grasping streak and partly to their extreme sentimentality, which invests every little item with enormous emotional significance. This grasping side of the Cancerian nature should be nipped in the bud early in life, and sharing toys and treats should be encouraged. Discipline can be hard for parents of Cancerians to maintain, especially if one or both of them are Crabs themselves, because the children take everything so much to heart and can become distressed even when mildly admonished. The best way of coping with them is by appealing directly to their love and loyalty: punishments do not need to be particularly severe.

Many Cancerian children are placid souls and, while not especially witty, can be amusing and imaginative. Cancerians are often timid and can develop an inferiority complex. Perversely, they sometimes become almost proud of this complex in later life, using it as an excuse not to take risks or improve themselves, intellectually or materially.

These children can often find it hard to cope with bereavement, whether that is the death of a pet or of a family member. They will see the death as a betrayal of love or an abandonment, and may become traumatized and angry with the departed. They should be encouraged to talk about their feelings.

Famous Cancerians

Alexander the Great

Diana, Princess of Wales

Rubens

George Orwell

O. J. Simpson

Meryl Streep

Louis Mountbatten

Emmeline Pankhurst

Marcel Proust

Arnold Schwarzenegger

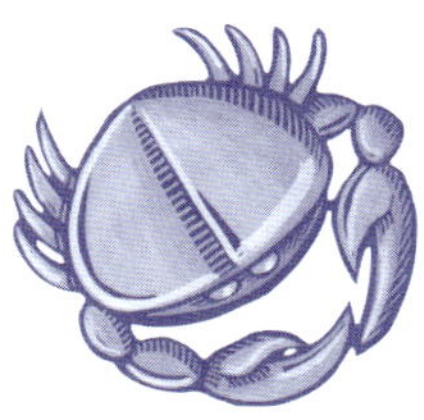

Julius Caesar

James Cagney

Louis Armstrong

Ginger Rogers

Jean Cocteau

King Henry VIII

Arlo Guthrie

Arthur Ashe

Nelson Rockefeller

Ernest Hemingway

Finding Your Sun Sign (2020 dates)

Aries	20 March–19 April*
Taurus	20 April–20 May
Gemini	21 May–20 June
Cancer	21 June–21 July
Leo	22 July–22 August
Virgo	23 August–22 September
Libra	23 September–22 October
Scorpio	23 October–21 November
Sagittarius	22 November–20 December
Capricorn	21 December–20 January
Aquarius	21 January–18 February
Pisces	19 February–19 March

*The dates provided in this book reflect the year 2020.
Dates may vary by a day or two from year to year.